Basics

half-hitch knot

Come out a bead and form a loop perpendicular to the thread between beads. Bring the needle under the thread away from the loop. Then go back over the thread and through the loop. Pull gently so the knot doesn't tighten prematurely.

surgeon's knot

Cross the right end over the left and go through the loop. Go through the loop again. Pull the ends to tighten. Cross the left end over the right end and go through once. Tighten.

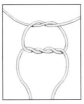

flattened crimp

1 Hold the crimp bead using the tip of your chainnose pliers. Squeeze the pliers firmly to flatten the crimp. Tug the clasp to make sure the crimp has a solid grip on the wire. If the wire slides, remove the crimp bead and repeat the steps with a new crimp bead.

2 Test to make sure the flattened crimp is secure.

plain loop

1 Trim the wire ⅜ in. (1cm) above the top bead. Make a right-angle bend close to the bead.

2 Grab the wire's tip with roundnose pliers. Roll the wire to form a half circle. Release the wire.

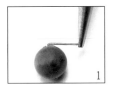 

3 Reposition the pliers in the loop and continue rolling, forming a centered circle above the bead.

4 The finished loop should have a nicely rounded shape.

wrapped loop

1 Make sure you have at least 1¼ in. (3.2cm) of wire above the bead. With the tip of your chainnose pliers, grasp the wire directly above the bead. Bend the wire above the pliers into a right angle.

2 Using roundnose pliers, position the jaws vertically in the bend.

3 Bring the wire over the top jaw of the roundnose pliers.

4 Keep the jaws vertical and reposition the pliers' lower jaw snugly into the loop. Curve the wire downward around the bottom of the roundnose pliers. This is the first half of a wrapped loop.

5 Position the chainnose pliers' jaws across the loop.

6 Wrap the wire around the wire stem, covering the stem between the loop and the top of the bead. Trim the excess wire and press the cut end close to the wraps with chainnose pliers.

opening a jump ring

1 Hold the jump ring with two pairs of chainnose pliers or chainnose and roundnose pliers, as shown.

2 To open the jump ring, bring the tips of one pair of pliers toward you and push the tips of the other pair away.

3 String materials on the open jump ring.

square stitch

1 String the required number of beads for the first row. Then string the first bead of the second row and go through the last bead of the first row and the first bead of the second row in the same direction. The new bead sits on top of the old bead and the holes are parallel.

2 String the second bead of row 2 and go through the next-to-last bead of row 1. Continue through the new bead of row 2. Repeat this step for the entire row.

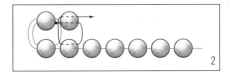

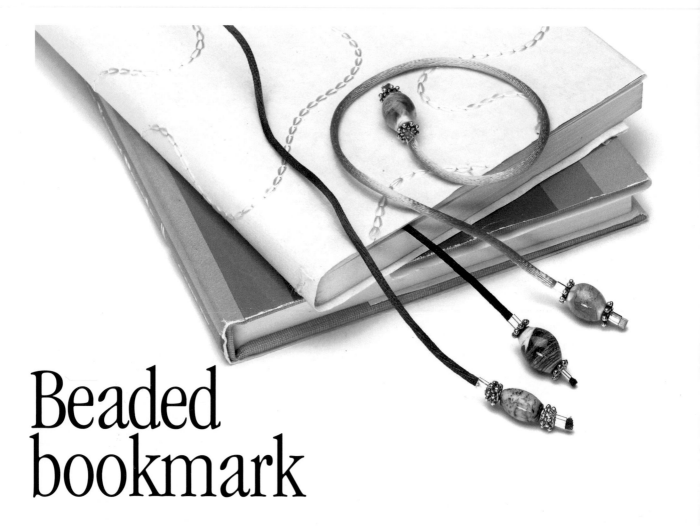

Beaded bookmark

These charming and easy-to-make bookmarks are a great way to display or share handmade beads. Create one to accompany the gift of a book, or make several to keep with your library.

❶ Cut a piece of satin cord approximately 2 in. (5cm) longer than your book's spine. Trim each end to a point and apply Fray Check (**photo a**). Let dry.

❷ String a crimp bead, a spacer, an art bead, a spacer, and a crimp bead close to one end of the cord (**photo b**).

❸ Flatten both crimps (see "Basics," p. 3) and trim any excess cord ¼ in. (6mm) from the crimp near the cord's end (**photo c**).

❹ Repeat steps 2 and 3 on the other end of the cord. ❍ – *Bonnie Propst*

materials
- **2** art beads, approx. 8 x 12mm
- **2** ft. (.61m) 1.5mm satin cord
- **4** 3mm flat spacers
- **4** 3mm crimp beads
- Dritz Fray Check

Tools: chainnose pliers

a

b

c

12 in./31cm

Wire critters

These whimsical earrings are simple to make and a great way to learn about working with wire. If you haven't done much wire work before, start with an inexpensive material, such as copper or craft wire. Then move on to gold-filled or sterling once you're comfortable with the tools and techniques. Follow the templates drawn by our illustrator, Kellie Jaeger, or sketch a few figures of your own.

❶ Choose a template and cut the appropriate length of wire. Bend the wire about 1½ in. (3.8cm) from one end.
❷ Using the bend as your starting point, manipulate the wire into the desired shape (**photo a**). Begin at the red dot on the template and use your fingers and tools to recreate the curves and angles of the design. Avoid bending the wire back and forth at any one spot or it will weaken and break.
❸ Complete the figure by wrapping the wire tail around the 1½-in. end twice (**photo b**). Keep the wraps close to the figure.
❹ With the 1½-in. wire end, make a wrapped or plain loop (see "Basics," p. 3) above the wraps made in step 3 (**photo c**). If you make a wrapped loop, continue wrapping until the two sets of wraps meet. Trim the excess wire.
❺ Once you have completed a figure, hammer it gently to harden the wire.
❻ To embellish the figure, string one or more beads on 24-gauge wire. Wrap one wire end tightly around the shaped wire, slide the bead or beads into position, and secure the remaining wire end with another few wraps. A drop of glue will hold the wraps in place.

a

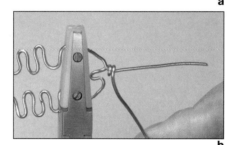

b

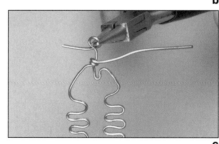

c

❼ Open the loop on an earring wire and attach the earring loop. Make a second earring to match or complement the first. ❍ – *Mindy Brooks*

12 in./31cm

10 in./25cm

12 in./31cm

materials

- 18-gauge wire (see templates for lengths)
- 18 in. (46cm) 24-gauge wire
- assorted 2-3mm beads
- **2** earring wires

Tools: roundnose and chainnose pliers, ball peen hammer, anvil, wire cutters

Optional: G-S Hypo Cement

Bead mosaic heart

Glue this mosaic heart to the corner of a photo frame, hang it, or attach a magnet to the back.

1 If you wish to hang your mosaic heart, screw an eyescrew in the center top of the heart.

2 Glue three or four seed beads, hole side up, in the center of the heart. Glue the flower centerpiece on top of these beads (**photo a**).

3 Glue leaf and/or fruit beads around the flower bead (**photo b**). Add a few 2mm or 3mm round beads to the flower and leaf arrangement (**photo c**).

4 Glue the foil-backed rhinestones around the heart's edge (**photo d**). Allow to dry until set.

5 Apply glue to a small portion of the exposed wood. Cut one end of a bead strand from the hank. Hold the beads on the strand and position the end of the strand in a line radiating from the heart's center to its edge in the glued section. Press the beads into the glue and pull out the string. Position another line of beads next to the first and repeat. Add lines of beads around the entire heart (**photo e**). Let the glue dry completely.

6 Apply a generous layer of glue to the heart's back. Cover the glued area with a mix of seed beads, leaving as little wood as possible exposed (**photo f**). Press the beads firmly into the glue and allow the piece to dry overnight.

7 Following the manufacturer's instructions, mix a small amount of grout. Adjust the mix to a consistency slightly looser than peanut butter.

8 Apply the grout to the entire piece (**photo g**). Set aside for about 15 minutes, allowing the grout to set between the beads. Remove the excess grout with an old toothbrush over a bucket of water (**photo h**). Rinse and brush repeatedly until the beads are

a

b

c

d

e

f

g

h

materials

- assorted seed, flower, leaf, and fruit beads
- hank seed beads
- foil-backed rhinestones
- 2 x 2 in. (5 x 5cm) wood heart (available at craft stores)
- Aleene's Thick Designer Tacky Glue
- unsanded polymer-modified wall tile grout
- Krylon Crystal Clear acrylic spray varnish, gloss finish

Tools: putty or plastic knife, toothbrush, disposable bucket

Optional: small eyescrew

exposed on the front and back. Let the heart dry overnight. Never dispose of excess grout or dirty water in a sink.

9 If any beads fell off while grouting, glue them back in place and allow the glue to dry. Use a cloth to remove any residue and polish the beads.

10 Spray the front and the back of the heart with varnish, applying three or four coats. Allow each coat to dry between applications. ●

– *Betsy Youngquist*

Stitched filigree box

Use glass flower and leaf beads to enhance delicate silver favor boxes. Give them as gifts, display them as party favors, or make some for yourself to use as containers for potpourri or jewelry.

You can use craft wire to attach the beads, but Fireline fishing line is much easier to work with, and stitching provides extra security for the beads. Use a 4-ft. (1.2m) length of Fireline so you only have to add thread once. To end, go under a stitch on the underside of the lid and tie off with several half-hitch knots (see "Basics," p. 3).

Because this is a freeform project, the number and placement of flowers and leaves are a personal choice. To give the appearance that your flowers and leaves are on a grassy surface, you may wish to try filling in the top of the box between the flowers and leaves with areas of green seed beads.

❶ Thread a twisted wire beading needle with 4 ft. of Fireline. Tie a seed bead on the end with a surgeon's knot (**photo a** and "Basics").
❷ Bring the needle up through a center hole of the box lid from the inside. String on a flower and a contrasting-color seed bead.
❸ Go back through the flower and the same hole (**photo b**). Tighten the stitch and come up a nearby hole.
❹ String seven to nine green seed beads and go back through the lid one hole away from where you came up (**photo c**). Tighten the thread and come up a nearby hole.
❺ String on a leaf and go back down the same hole (**photo d**).
❻ Repeat steps 2–5 to add flowers,

leaves, and grass (**photo e**) until the lid is completely covered.
❼ To give the underside of the lid a neat finish, trace around the lid on a piece of green felt. Cut out the tracing inside the lines so it just fits the inside. Glue in place with a few drops of tacky glue. ❂ – *Paulette Biedenbender*

materials

- favor box (Wilton, 800-794-5866, wilton.com, or JoAnn Fabrics)
- 30-40 8-13mm glass flower-shaped beads, various colors, shapes, and sizes
- 20-30 8mm Czech glass leaves
- 3g seed beads, size 11º, in three colors that contrast with flowers
- 3g seed beads, size 11º, green
- Fireline fishing line, 20 lb. test
- twisted wire beading needles

Optional: green felt, tacky glue

tip

Spilled beads

An adhesive lint roller is perfect for picking up stray beads. Just roll it over the surface where the beads fell, tear the sheet from the roll, and remove the beads from the tape.
– *Melissa Wisdom, Murfreesboro, TN*

a

b

c

d

e

Memory wire charm

Ring-sized memory wire holds its shape perfectly and can be used to create many small decorative embellishments: wineglass charms, cardholders, and more.

When cutting memory wire, be sure to use heavy-duty or memory-wire cutters; it will damage standard wire cutters. Alternatively, grasp the wire at the point you wish to cut it, and bend the wire back and forth several times until it snaps.

1 Cut a piece of memory wire three to five coils long. Use roundnose pliers to turn a loop at one end of the memory wire (**photo a**).
2 On the other end of the memory wire, string a 3mm bead, a 6mm bead, and another 3mm bead (**photo b**).
3 String a 4mm bead, a 6mm bead, and another 4mm bead (**photo c**).
4 Repeat steps 2 and 3 until all but one of the coils are strung with beads. End

with a 3mm bead (**photo d**).
5 String a charm, a 3mm bead, a 6mm bead, and a 3mm bead (**photo e**). You may need to add a jump ring to make the charm's loop face the right way. If so, open the jump ring (see "Basics," p. 3), slide the charm on, and close the loop.
6 Repeat step 3 to finish the coil, leaving a ¼-½-in. (6-13mm) wire tail. Turn a loop at the end of the memory wire. **○** – *Kristin Schneidler*

materials

one charm
- **5-7** coils ring-sized memory wire
- **50-100** 3mm, 4mm, and 6mm fire-polished beads
- decorative charm
- small jump ring

Tools: chainnose pliers, roundnose pliers, memory-wire or heavy-duty wire cutters

a

b

c

d

e

Pearl and wire cuff links

An understated blouse speaks volumes when its cuffs are adorned with pearl-clustered links. This pair of cuff links is a versatile addition to your jewelry wardrobe and might be all you need to move your classic suit from drab to fab.

❶ String nine head pins with a 6mm pearl, and nine head pins with a crystal and a 4mm pearl. Make a wrapped loop (see "Basics," p. 3) on each head pin above the top bead (**photo a**).

❷ Cut an 8-in. (20cm) piece of wire and make the first half of a wrapped loop 1½ in. (3.8cm) from one end. Make your loop 3-4mm in diameter to accommodate all the pearl units (**photo b**).

❸ Slide the pearl units onto the loop, alternating styles. Complete one wrap and trim the excess wire (**photo c**).

❹ Slide a flat bead and a spacer onto the wire (**photo d**).

❺ Bend the wire at a right angle ½ in. (1.3cm) from the spacer (**photo e**, p. 10). (Adjust the length for a longer or shorter cuff link.)

❻ Make the first half of a wrapped loop and slide on a toggle end (**photo f**).

❼ Complete the wraps down the length of the wire until flush with the spacer. Trim the excess wire (**photo g**). Make a second cuff link to match the first. ●

– Lynne Dixon-Speller

c

d

a

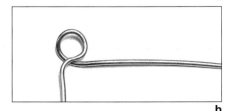

b

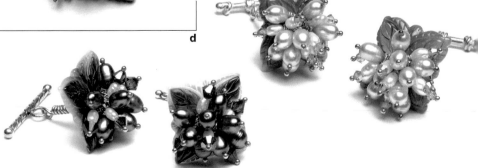

materials

- 16-in. (41cm) strand 6mm rice-shaped freshwater pearls
- 16-in. strand 4mm rice-shaped freshwater pearls
- 18 4mm bicone crystals
- 2 20mm square center-drilled mother-of-pearl flat beads (Eclectica, 262-641-0910)
- 2 6mm flat spacers
- 36 1½-in. (3.8cm) decorative head pins
- 2 toggle bars
- 16 in. 20-gauge wire

Tools: chainnose pliers, roundnose pliers, diagonal wire cutters

Beaded hair ornaments

Every day can be a good hair day with beaded hair accessories. The ponytail holder and barrettes both use the basic technique of wiring beads to the base. For the ponytail holder, I used Czech fire-polished beads because they are available in a variety of complementary shades. For the barrettes, I created a monochromatic palette, combining gemstone chips with 4mm Swarovski crystals in a similar color.

ponytail holder

❶ Open the ponytail clip by squeezing it gently; this will prevent you from accidentally wiring the clip shut. Be sure to thread the wire under protruding parts of the base.

❷ Thread the wire through the hole in one end of the ponytail clip, leaving a 1-in. (2.5cm) tail. Using your fingers, twist the tail and working wire together tightly four times. Trim the excess wire from the tail (**photo a**).

❸ Thread the wire through two beads, sliding the beads over the twisted

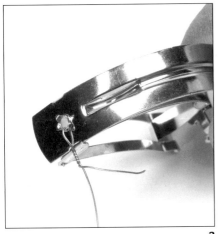

a

c

e

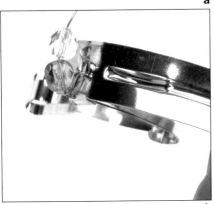

b

d

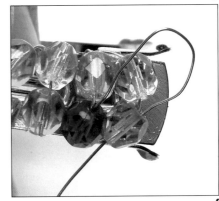

f

section of the wire (**photo b**).

❹ Wrap the wire firmly around the ponytail holder twice to anchor the beads to the clip (**photo c**).

❺ Continue adding two beads at a time, alternating a main color with other colors. Wrap the wire around the ponytail base once between each pair of beads to secure them without revealing excess wire (**photo d**).

❻ After you cover the clip with beads, wrap the wire around the base between the last two pairs of beads (**photo e**).

❼ Thread the wire up through a nearby bead, then down through an adjacent bead (**photo f**). Trim the excess wire.

barrette

Use 28-gauge wire, which will pass through small gemstone holes easily. You may also temporarily remove the U-shaped bar on the barrette to avoid wiring it to the base. Follow the instructions for the ponytail holder, alternating gemstone and bicone bead pairs. Replace the U-shaped bar. ❂

– Naomi Fujimoto

materials

ponytail holder
- **30** 6mm Czech fire-polished beads (clear, aqua, cobalt, and light blue)
- 3½-in. (8.75cm) ponytail clip (Rio Grande, 800-545-6566)
- 26-gauge craft wire, silver

barrette
- **11** 5mm gemstone chips (carnelian, turquoise, or citrine)
- **11** 4mm crystal bicone beads (Swarovski light topaz, blue zircon, or citrine cathedral)
- 2-in. (5cm) French barrette
- 28-gauge craft wire, silver

both projects
Tools: diagonal wire cutters

③ Open the loop on an earring wire
and attach the tree. Close the earring
wire's loop (**photo g**). Make a second
earring to match the first.

angel necklace

❶ String a 6mm square spacer or
rondelle, a triangle, wings, a round, and
a flat spacer on a head pin (**photo h**).

❷ Above the top bead, make a wrapped
loop large enough to accommodate the
ribbon (**photo i**).

❸ Determine the finished length of
your necklace. (This one is 16 in./41cm.)
Add 1 in. and cut a piece of ribbon to
that length. Thread the ribbon through
the loop and center the pendant on the
ribbon (**photo j**).

❹ Knot one end of the ribbon and
place the knot in the crimp end. Glue
the knot (**photo k**). Fold down the sides
of the crimp end and squeeze gently
with chainnose pliers. Repeat on the
other end. Trim the excess ribbon.

❺ Attach a split ring to one crimp end
and attach a lobster claw clasp to the
split ring (**photo l**). Repeat on the other
end to add a split ring. ● – *Mary Krohn,
Erika Hipp, and Sydney Smith*

a

b

Holiday dangles

Add sparkle to your season with
a spunky snowman, a twinkling
tree, or an ethereal angel. Each
project uses just a few beads and
components. Whether you present them
to friends, use them to decorate a gift, or
keep them for yourself, these projects are
sure to spark holiday spirit.

snowman earrings

❶ String a 3mm round bead on a 1-in.
(2.5cm) head pin. Make a wrapped
loop (see "Basics," p. 3), leaving about
2mm between the bead and the wraps
(**photo a**).

❷ String a flat spacer, an 8mm round,
the bead unit from step 1, a 6mm crystal
rondelle, a 7mm round, a 5mm rondelle,
and a cylinder bead onto a 2-in. (5cm)
head pin (**photo b**).

❸ Make a wrapped loop above the top
bead (**photo c**).

❹ Open the loop on an earring wire
and attach the snowman. Close the
earring wire's loop (**photo d**). Make
a second earring to match the first.

Christmas tree earrings

❶ String a rondelle, a cone, and a
bicone on a head pin (**photo e**).

❷ Make a wrapped loop above the top
bead (**photo f**).

c

g

d

h

e

i

f

j

materials

snowman earrings

- **2** 8mm round beads, stardust
- **2** 7mm round beads, stardust
- **2** 6mm rondelles, multicolor crystal
- **2** 5mm rondelles, black
- **2** size 8º Japanese cylinder beads, black
- **2** 3mm fire-polished round beads
- **2** 4mm flat spacers
- **2** 1-in. (2.5cm) head pins
- **2** 2-in. (5cm) head pins
- earring wires

Christmas tree earrings

- **2** 10mm Murano glass cones, green
- **2** 6mm rondelles, multicolor crystal
- **2** 4mm bicone crystals
- **2** 1½-in. (3.8cm) head pins
- earring wires

angel necklace

- 15mm Murano glass triangle, white
- 5 x 15mm center-drilled wings
- 6mm Murano glass round or
  5mm pearl, white
- 6mm square spacer or rondelle
- 6mm flat spacer
- 2-in. head pin
- **2** crimp ends
- 2 ft. (61cm) ribbon
- lobster claw clasp and **2** split rings
- G-S Hypo Cement

all projects

Tools: chainnose and roundnose pliers,
diagonal wire cutters
Optional: split-ring pliers

*Contact Funky Hannah's at 262-634-6088 to
purchase kits for these projects.*

k

l

Wire macramé ring

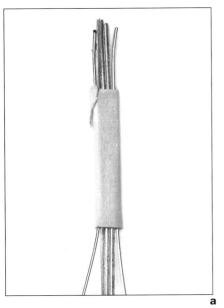

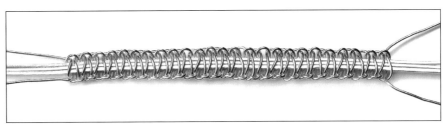

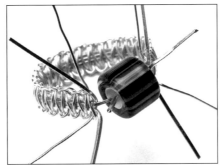

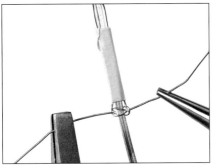

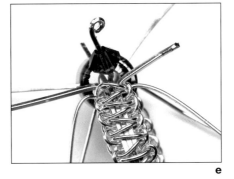

making macramé square knots

1 Cross the right-hand knotting cord (rh) over the core and the left-hand knotting cord (lh) under the core. This creates a loop between each cord and the core. Pass the rh cord through the loop on the left from front to back and the lh cord through the loop on the right from back to front.

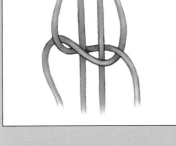

2 Reverse the steps to make the second half of the knot: Cross the lh cord over the core and the rh cord under the core. Pass the lh cord through the loop on the right from from to back and the rh cord through the loop on the left from back to front.

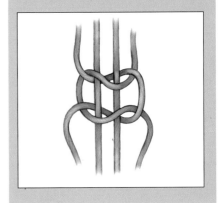

Combine two types of wire with a few beads to make this fun and funky ring. Make sure your 24-gauge wire is dead soft—anything harder won't work.

1 Cut the square wire into three 4-in. (10cm) pieces.

2 Cut the 24-gauge wire into two 18-in. (46cm) pieces and place one on each side of the group of square wires. Tape the five wires together about ½ in. (1.2cm) from the top (**photo a**).

3 Measure the widest part of your finger or use a ring mandrel to determine the desired circumference of your ring. Subtract the length of the focal bead from the circumference.

4 With the two pieces of 24-gauge wire, make a macramé square knot (**sidebar**) around the group of square wires (**photo b**). Pull the wire ends with pliers to make the knot snug.

5 Continue making square knots until the knotted portion reaches the length determined in step 3, minus the focal bead length (**photo c**).

6 When the band is long enough, remove the tape and shape the band around a cylindrical form. Go through the focal bead with both ends of the center square wire (**photo d**).

7 Trim the wire ends to ⅜ in. (1cm). String a 2-4mm bead on one of the wire ends. With roundnose pliers, make a tiny loop at the very end of the wire (**photo e**). Compress the loop and coil the rest of the wire around it. Press the coil against the small bead (**photo f**). Repeat with the matching wire on the other side of the focal bead.

8 Repeat step 7 with the eight remaining wires. ● – *Julia Gerlach*

materials
- 1 ft. (31cm) 22-gauge sterling silver square wire
- 3 ft. (.9m) 24-gauge sterling silver round wire, dead soft
- focal bead with large hole
- 10 assorted 2-3mm accent beads

Tools: roundnose and chainnose pliers, wire cutters, ring mandrel or other cylindrical form

Magical dragonflies

Make these enchanting dragonfly sculptures with beads, wire, and silk thread; their variations are limited only by the available bead and thread colors.

First construct the dragonfly's body, then add the wing details. Finally, embellish the dragonfly with beads.

the body

1 Cut the wire into three 6-in. (15cm) lengths. Bend two of the wires around the dowel at their centers for the wings. Bend the third around the roundnose pliers at its center for the body (**photo a**).

2 Bend the ends of the wires up, perpendicular to the rest of the wire, 1 in. (2.5cm) from the end to form legs.

3 Lay the body wire vertically on a work surface with the legs at the top. Place the wing wires perpendicular to the body, legs together, forming a T shape. Tape all three pieces in position. Spread the legs out and push them down so they are at a 45-degree angle to the body wire (**photo b**).

4 Wrap the end of the floss around the legs in a circle and tie to secure. *Bring the floss over the closest leg. Wrap under and around the leg. Pull tight and move to the next leg (**figure 1, p. 18**, and **photo c**). Repeat from * around until the legs are securely held in place.

5 Hold the floss in position and pull the tape off. Hold the dragonfly in one hand with the legs toward you and wrap a figure 8 around the wings: Go under

the bottom of the right wing, then up and over its top. Go under the body and the left wing. Bring the floss over the left wing and under the body and right wing. Come over the right wing (**figure 2**). Repeat this figure 8 until the thorax is built up and the wings are secure, ending near the tail of the dragonfly. The wings will move a little when pushed but should stand alone.

6 Wrap the floss around the tail until it's covered. Keep the wraps side by side —close and tight—(**photo d**) for a smooth finish with no gaps.

7 When you reach the tail's end, cut the floss from the spool or skein, leaving an 8-in. (20cm) tail. Work half-hitch knots (see "Basics," p. 3) around the arc at the tail's end to cover the metal. Keep them close together (**figure 3**).

wing detail

1 Thread a needle with 2 yd. (1.8m) of the finer thread. Tie one end onto the fibers along the side of the body inside the base of the wing. Pass the needle under and around the wire of a wing ½ to ¾ in. (1.3 to 2cm) from the floss. Pass the needle through the loop that forms and pull tight. Run the needle under and over the wire approximately ¼ in. (6mm) away and come through the loop. Repeat around the edge of the wing. When you reach the opposite side, sew through the fibers on the side of the body and tie a knot.

2 Begin the next row by sewing under the thread between the first two half-

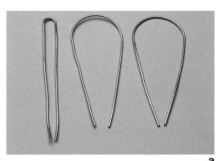
a

b

c

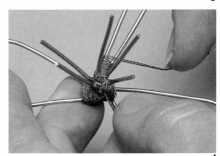
d

hitch knots of the previous row and making a half-hitch; continue around (**figure 3**). End by tying onto the body fibers as before. Work as many rows as needed to fill in the lacy wing, leaving a space in the center to give the impression of two wings. If the space is too small, consider adding a strand of beads to split the wings.

3 Repeat steps 1-2 on the other wing.

4 Thread a needle with 1 yd. (.9m) of Fireline. Tie a thread to the top center of the body. String two or three seed beads, an 8mm bead, and two seed beads. Skip the last two seed beads and sew back through the 8mm bead and the other seed beads. Secure the thread and clip (**photo e**).

5 String enough seed beads to make a circle around the beads below the head. Tie into a circle. Work a row of one-bead square stitch (see "Basics") around the circle to fill in the space between the 8mm bead and the body (**figure 4**). Work two-bead square stitch down the body (**figure 5**).

6 String 2-3 in. (5-7.6cm) of seed beads and wrap them around the tail (**photo f**). Secure the end with several half-hitch knots. ● – *Sharon Bateman*

e

f

materials

- 2g assorted seed beads, size 14º or 12º
- 8mm bead or crystal
- embroidery floss, approx. 3 yd. (2.7m)
- multicolored rayon/silk thread for needlelace wings
- Fireline fishing line, 10 lb. test
- 18 in. (46cm) 18-gauge copper or brass wire
- 1-in. (2.5cm) dowel
- beading needles, #12 or 13

Tools: wire cutters, roundnose pliers, chainnose pliers, scissors, tape

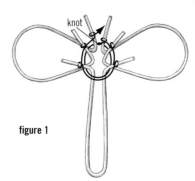
figure 1

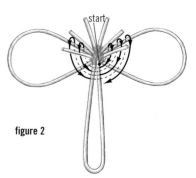
figure 2

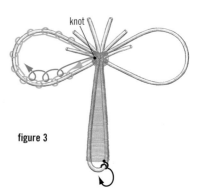
figure 3

figure 4

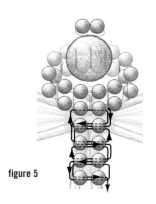
figure 5

tip

Needle attraction

When I first started working with seed beads, I was flabbergasted by how fine the beading needles are. While I had no trouble putting the needle through those tiny beads, I had a horrible time trying to pick up the needle in the first place. To solve the problem, I ran a strong magnet over one of my metal tools. Now when I need to pick up a needle, I simply pass the tool over the needle and the needle hops on the tool, allowing me to pick it up with ease.
– *Kimberly Szalkiewicz, Escondido, CA*

Contributors

Bead artist and sculptor **Sharon Bateman** has written several beading books and has had her designs published in various beading magazines. She has appeared on *Jewelry Making* (DIY Network) and manufactures and sells a line of specialized tube and peyote looms. Visit her website at sharonbateman.com.

Paulette Biedenbender owns Bead Needs, LLC in Hales Corners, Wisconsin. She has been beading for more than 10 years, and enjoys designing amulet bag patterns and teaching new beaders how to bead.

Mindy Brooks is editor of *Bead&Button* magzaine and founding editor of *BeadStyle* magazine.

Lynne Dixon-Speller is a frequent contributor to *BeadStyle* magazine.

Naomi Fujimoto is an associate editor with *BeadStyle* magazine.

Julia Gerlach is an associate editor with Kalmbach Books.

Bonnie Propst
Making and collecting beads have always been passions of Bonnie's. She enjoys the unique and varied results that come from making enamel beads, and uses materials from nature and the sea to inspire and complement her designs. Using her beads in functional and wearable projects, such as bookmarks and jewelry, brings her much joy. Bonnie's beads are available for sale; contact her at bonniebead@juno.com.

Mary Krohn and **Erica Hipp** are employees of Funky Hannah's Beads and Art in Racine, Wisconsin; **Sydney Smith** is Mary's 5-year-old granddaughter.

Betsy Youngquist has participated in art fairs, juried art exhibitions, and invitational shows nationwide. She has been using a beaded mosaic process to cover forms since 1995. Visit her website at byart.com.

Get Great Jewelry Projects All Through the Year

finishing touches

A complete high intermediate course in English

Volume B

Samuela Eckstut-Didier

PRENTICE HALL INTERNATIONAL ENGLISH LANGUAGE TEACHING